A. Dane

3 Days in Copenhagen

Copenhagen Travel Guide – Best 72 Hours in Copenhagen for First-Timers

First edition

Contents

I

Introduction

"I've always liked being able to go around incognito in Copenhagen."

- Sandi Toksvig

1

Hej med dig! (Hi There!)

It's very exciting that you are going to Copenhagen, which happens to be one of my favorite big cities and also my hometown for the last 30 odd years. I'll do my best to prepare you for a stay of a lifetime within a reasonable budget. I'll cover what I believe you will need to know, such as when best to go to Copenhagen, how to choose where to stay, what to do and see, the gems, timesaving and money saving tips as well as my personal and the locals' general favorites in the city.

Copenhagen is a popular tourist destination, and even more so these years it seems. It's actually been voted the number one city in the world to travel to in 2019.[1] That being said, my intention with this guide is not to display a picturesque and glamorous picture of a city that real life could never live up to. In fact, I will be careful not to create expectations that inevitably will end in disappointment. I have seen and heard this happen too often myself. In my experience, the best trips have been the ones I have researched the least, where I have steered clear of people's excitement and optimistic opinions prior to my own departure. This might seem counterintuitive since I'm writing a guide book. However, I will try not to hype and form a fixed image of Copenhagen in your mind. My intention is to provide valuable tips with as much bang for the buck as possible. I will lay out a realistic and intuitive itinerary for your inspiration and necessary planning within the limited amount of time.

Three days doesn't really seem like quite enough time for what any intriguing capital has to offer. It could, however, be a reasonable amount of time for experiencing the best of Copenhagen *if* you have a clear, workable plan and *if* you apply time-saving strategies. This guide provides a thorough 3-day itinerary that is actually realistic and will get you through the must-see and best attractions in Copenhagen in a suitable order.

---

[1] By Lonely Planet

I haven't included and randomly picked a lot of sites you *could* see, but there are obviously a lot of those. I have carefully selected only the sights and areas I believe provide a valuable experience for most people and that you *should* see. I have created a must-see 3-day itinerary that is intuitively put together with the least amount of transportation between places. Hence, this guide provides the best of the best of Copenhagen in the most time-efficient manner. Quite clever if I might add.

More so, it provides descriptions and recommendations, what to add, should you spend more days, how to explore Copenhagen if traveling with kids, and how to best stay and thrive in Copenhagen.

I have consecutively included addresses, opening hours, and links to websites should you want to read more.

Even though Copenhagen is not exactly the cheapest city on the planet, the high-end capital can be experienced in 3 days within a reasonable budget. Many of the suggested must-see sites are in fact free. However, it's easy to spend money, and if you want to get the full Noma dining experience, go all-in with shopping and what not then obviously set aside a bit of cash in advance. On that note, I fully believe that an extraordinary city experience doesn't have to be expensive to be great. Rather than seeking fine cuisine and Instagram-worthy scenery how about doing some experimental traveling? I believe in making memories not checklists, eating street food and going for picnics in the park, seeing cultural sights from different angels and outside rush hours. And perhaps most importantly, prepare to quit the itinerary when spontaneity calls for action. What do you think?

How to Use This Book as Your Guide

I have divided this book into two main parts. The first part consists of my suggested 3-day must-see itinerary along with pieces of information about the places to visit in Copenhagen.

The second part contains pertinent information about Danish culture and etiquette along with recommendations on where to stay, what to eat, where to shop, etc. I have included some handy information such as neighborhood descriptions and distance from the city center which should allow you to decide on the area to stay if you have not yet booked accommodation.

I suggest that you use the book for generally planning your stay and sketching up how to spend your days. I have created the must-see itinerary as a plug-and-play plan, but it also works great for inspiration to get an idea of how much you can realistically cover in one as well as all three days.

2

Why Should You Visit Copenhagen?

This book is obviously not the first you have ever heard of Copenhagen, and you probably don't need reasons to choose Copenhagen as your next destination. However, I want to include some of the features that make Copenhagen stand out and things to notice while you are there. So here goes.

In addition to its rich culture, heritage, and history, Copenhagen has other reasons for being a highly visited tourist attraction. In general, the city has managed to retain its historical charm while imbibing the trendy attitude of the modern world leaving you feeling satiated for having leveraged the benefits of both.

Hans Christian Andersen is the first name that usually strikes people's minds when they think or talk of Denmark and its capital city, Copenhagen. Denmark, in general, and Copenhagen, in particular, have obviously more to them than the famous fairy tale author, and in daily life, he doesn't take up a lot of space. But the great man's persona and his characters can be seen and felt all across the country and the city in glimpses.

The Land of Hygge and Happiness

Denmark has multiple times been voted the happiest country in the world, and the world-famous "hygge" is a Danish concept. Not a single day goes by where a Dane does not embrace in hygge. They always bring hygge into their daily lives. Hygge is essentially a feeling of wellbeing that plays a huge part of the everyday lifestyle of Copenhageners. For this reason alone, Copenhagen should be a bucket-list no brainer. I invite you to embrace hygge as much as possible during your stay, and I will provide some ideas for you. Hygge could be one of the best things you could bring with you back home.

The City of Designs

Danish people love quality and Denmark is famous for their classic designs especially in regard to furniture. When it comes to design, Danes take a need for perfection and high quality a few notches up. Scandinavian design is world famous for its stylish minimalism with Copenhagen being one of the leading cities. In many furniture shops, big or small, you will find an amazing range of designs right from the classic to the contemporary, and in the city picture, you will come across these designs in public here and there.

Dedicated Bike Lanes and Designated Bike Paths

Copenhagen is, perhaps, one of the few cities in the world that has integrated dedicated paths for bikers. The Danes take cycling very seriously, and entire sections of the roads are cordoned off just for bikes making cycling one of the most wonderful and also safe ways of getting around the city. The sight of so many people on their cycles going about their days creates a sense of bonhomie that is unparalleled. Take part in this on a bike which is a great way to get around. Copenhagen also has many designated bike paths where you can explore the city on a bike separated from motorized traffic.

Be aware of the official and unofficial rules for participating in traffic on a bike. Danes are almost perfidious about bike rules, and I'm honestly no exception myself. I'll let you in on these "rules" further down below.

Outstandingly Delicious Food

Home to a Mecca of restaurants, Noma, Copenhagen's food journey creates gastronomic delights for anyone who wants to savor it. Yes, Noma Restaurant might be out of reach for budget travelers, but there is no doubt that its extremely high standards in the realm of eating and dining out have cascaded down. Most eateries in Copenhagen, irrespective of budget and location, strive to achieve outstanding levels in preparing and serving delicious foods under hygienic conditions.

There are delicious street foods available at several markets that have popped up in Copenhagen over the last few decades. The food places serve all kinds of dishes, including but not limited to seafood varieties, gourmet chocolates, meats, cheeses, breads, coffees, salads, and of course, the Danish pastry. I will go into more details about Copenhagen street food later.

While the Danish pastry has traveled all over the world today, the ones you get in Copenhagen have their own unique flavor that is difficult to replicate. The Danish pastry, especially in Copenhagen, has had a sort of quality renaissance over the past years, and the new bakeries such as Lagkagehuset serve high-level delicious pastries that the Danes absolutely love. It's a bit pricy but worth it.

The Copenhagen Palaces

No matter how contemporary your outlook is, there is nothing more endearing about a history class than a visit to palaces and castles that tell tales of valor, romance, and love. Copenhagen is known as the city of towers. The main palaces in the city (more about them later) and a couple of them outside Copenhagen are bound to stun you with their elaborate carvings, unmatched design of rooms and towers, and a cornucopia of historical artifacts and information.

One of the Safest Cities in the World

Young, old, single, couple, family, male, female. Copenhagen is as safe as it can be for all types of tourist constellations. The general assumption is that everybody can walk around freely and safely day and night all over town. However, there is a "but" here. Like every other big city, Copenhagen has pickpockets and other criminal elements. The crime rate is somewhat moderate, and if you don't take normal precautions such as being aware of your surrounding and closing your pockets firmly, you could be the victim of a crime. So just be sure to be attentive and you should be fine.

Progressive and Flourishing City

Copenhagen has fully put the recession behind her, and she is again flourishing. New and interesting buildings and even entirely new neighborhoods such as Nordhavn are popping up here and there. Fascinating and creative projects are being launched such as CopenHill – an energy plant which provides energy and waste treatment as well as being an architectural landmark and a leisure facility for actual skiing in the city. Innovation and environmental responsibility seem to be the buzz words of Copenhagen these years.

3

When to Visit Copenhagen

Summer months are definitely a prime time to visit Copenhagen and all of Scandinavia for that matter. I personally can't imagine a better city to stay in than Copenhagen during the summer months. There is a very special vibe, and there are so many wonderful spots to hang out and hygge. Harbor baths and beaches lie quite close to the city center, which makes summertime in Copenhagen even more pleasurable and diverse.

Already in spring around late April when the weather gets warmer, the vibe changes and the city really come to life. It's amazing to witness how all the Copenhageners come out and play at the first sight of warmth and sunlight.

If you are a winter travel buff, then Copenhagen is, perhaps, the best place to visit among all other Scandinavian cities considering that most of the time the temperatures hovers around the freezing point with occasional dips up to -15 degrees C. In winter, Copenhageners really turn on the hygge atmosphere with beautiful lights and decorations especially in Tivoli Gardens and around Kongens Nytorv, and you can experience a very authentic Copenhagen also with much fewer tourist. However, Copenhagen is never completely overrun by tourist like for instance Rome and Paris, so you will find space around you and probably not crazy long lines for the attractions even in summer. Hint: Many Copenhageners leave the city for traveling in July, as most actually have time off work here. There will be fewer crowds this month but probably also more tourists.

The months of October-November + January-April are probably the least exciting months to visit Copenhagen mainly because of the weather and that they are the general off-season time of year.

4

A Brief History Class

Knowing a bit of history about the place you are traveling to not only makes you more knowledgeable but also adds lots of detailed layers to your traveling experience as you make contact, see and feel everything you have read about in books. It's not within the scope of this book to provide detailed historical data, but here goes a very brief history brush-up of Copenhagen.

Copenhagen is the capital of Denmark and is the biggest city in Scandinavia. It is the home of the royal family together with around 1 million citizens.

Its Latin name is Hafnia, and its Danish name is København. With an area covering approximately 1980 square kilometers, Copenhagen was established during the period 1160-1167. It was designed and built by Bishop Absalon, under the order and auspices of King Valdemar I.

Bishop Absalon's order was to build a city on Sealand's east coast. This city was built with the intention of protecting the trade of the country in that area. Bishop Absalon built a small fortress on Slotsholmen Isle, and this was the beginning of the building of Copenhagen. By the 12th and 13th century, this little fishing village became a bustling city, and by the 15th century, Copenhagen became the capital city of Denmark replacing the earlier one, Roskilde.

II

The 3-Day Copenhagen Must-See Itinerary

"To travel is to live."

- Hans Christian Andersen

Three days can be sufficient for a wholesome visit both for those who like to take it slow and relaxed and for those who love to pack in as much as possible. I'll try to cater to both preferences.

The 3-Day Copenhagen Must-See Itinerary is a collection of the essential and important sights. These are the sight that shouldn't be missed or should at least be highly prioritized when visiting Copenhagen. They are all located within the city center or very close there to it.

I have made the Copenhagen Must-See Itinerary relaxed and realistic so that the sights can fit into each day with no hassle. If you want a more action-packed itinerary, you can add more from the "Extra if More Time"—suggestions found in the later chapters of this book. I have paid close attention to prioritizing the most important sight in this itinerary.

The itinerary is a mix of actual landmarks such as important monuments as well as neighborhood strolling.

Walking some of the neighborhoods of Copenhagen is absolutely not to be missed. One of the best experiences of any big city, in my opinion, is to experience the neighborhoods from street level. While classic tourist attractions are amazing and fun, simply strolling the neighborhoods provides a different and authentic city experience. While walking in the footsteps of the locals, you get to see the city through their eyes, and you get a glimpse of the daily lives.

Copenhagen has numerous neighborhoods. I consider Christianshavn, Nørrebro, København K (the city center) and Vesterbro to be especially noteworthy with their unique features. The itinerary includes strolling these particular neighborhoods.

If you have ever done big city tourism, you know that you should prepare for a lot of walking. It can be done with less walking, but it is undoubtedly the best way to experience any European capital and Copenhagen is no exception. Combining walking with bicycling and bus tours is a good way to lessen the overload on your feet.

The main sights in the itinerary can easily be done within the amount of time at hand. If you wish to see as much as possible, the suggestions marked as "Extra if More Time" are my best recommendations. These extra suggestions are included chronologically as well because of their location. So, for instance, if you wish to see "Our Savior's Church" you might as well include it while you are at Christianshavn, thus it is included in the itinerary right after Christianshavn.

5

Day 1 – København K, Christianshavn, Vesterbro

1. Rundetårn (The Round Tower)

I recommend starting your sightseeing by visiting Rundetårn on day 1. Rundetårn is a great historical sight, fun to climb, and provides a great view and first impression of the city from above. Rundetårn is a round observatory tower located in the center of Copenhagen, København K. The tower is known for having no stairs (except for at the top) but instead an upward-going spiral walking path. The tower was built by King Christian 4, as part of a church with the intent to provide access to the university library on top of the church as well as access to the university's astronomical observatory at the very top of the tower.

Rundetårn is located in the midst of Copenhagen city center, and from there you can enjoy a walk down the shopping street Købmagergade which is the way to the second must-see sight on day 1.

How much time: Set aside at least 1 hour for climbing the tower and enjoying the view.

Source: Google Maps

2. Christiansborg Palace

Secondly on day 1, I recommend visiting The Christiansborg Palace, which is within walking distance from Rundetårn (about 500 m; an 8-minute walk). This wondrous palace was once the principal home to the Danish kings, and today it's the home of the Danish parliament. While a part of it is still used by the extant Danish royal family, it has today become a symbol of democracy holding the legislative, executive, and judicial powers of the country.

Whether you are an art lover or a history buff or want to get the local flavor or a seeker of some peace and quiet, Christiansborg Palace will have something for you. Replete with historical information about the Danish monarchy, filled with amazingly beautiful architecture, the cradle of the present-day Danish political power and some great artworks all beckon every kind of traveler.

The Parliament, referred to as "Folketinget," can be visited only with an approved guide which must be booked in advance. However, other parts of the palace can be visited on your own without having to hire a guide. Other than the parliament house, you will be able to see the stables, the royal reception rooms including the Oval Throne Room and the Tower Room, the museum, the royal kitchen, and the old ruins—all of which are extremely worthy of exploring.

English guided tours at the parliament take place every day at 11 a.m. or 1 p.m. except Friday and Sunday.

How much time: You will need about two hours to complete the entire place, and it does make sense to use the services of a guide and visit the parliament as well.

3. Christiania and Christianshavn (Neighborhood Strolling)

Free of charge

Next up I recommend going to the neighborhood Christianshavn and more specifically Christiania free town, which is located at Christianshavn.

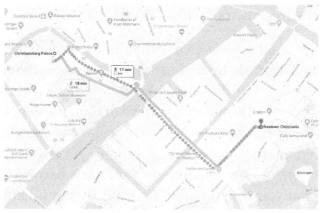

Source: Google Maps

Christiania

Christiania lies 2.5 km away from Christianborg Palace, and it takes around 30 min. to walk the distance. I recommend hopping on the bus 2A as it takes you directly from Christiansborg Palace to Christianshavn Metro

Station. And from there, you walk the rest of the way to Christiania – around 7 minutes of walking.

Christania can actually be categorized as both a landmark and a neighborhood. It is truly a unique area not similar to anything else in the western world to my knowledge. It is the closest you may get to some sort of permanent anarchy in Europe. Even though closing down the area has been a political agenda for decades and the police often carry out raids to close down the illegal marijuana sales, the free town remains intact to this date.

Visiting Christiania is a colorful and exciting experience indeed. The free town has a somewhat autonomous lifestyle that is officially obliged to follow the rules, regulations, and stipulated culture of Copenhagen, but in reality, they follow their own set of rules to some degree. Founded in 1971 by a set of hippies, Christiania was formed on old and abandoned military barracks, and today many are the houses are built by the inhabitants themselves.

Christiana is a society within a society and is open for visits from the public. It is a free town in the true sense of the word, and a visit to Christiania could open new vistas for you.

Be aware that it is prohibited to take pictures in Christiania and the inhabitants take this very seriously.

How much time: You could stay anywhere from 1 hour to half a day or more for a visit to Christiana.

Christianshavn (Neighborhood Strolling)

Christianshavn is a remarkable neighborhood that has a lot of history and yet is a very hip part of Copenhagen today. At present, Christianshavn is the most expensive neighborhood in Copenhagen for apartment-buying and thus the most popular area to live in. There are always lots of people on the streets, and you will get many different impressions when walking around Christianshavn. Once a borough of its own, Christianshavn is surrounded by water and boats frequently sail through the canals of this marvelous yet humble part of Copenhagen. You could easily find a café to enjoy a coffee or lunch close to the canal. The heart of Christianshavn is Christianshavns Torv, where you can also find the metro station. From there I suggest you cross the street and continue along the canal. Within a couple of minutes, you pass Our Savior's church on the right-hand side.

Extra if More Time: Our Savior's Church

If you feel like packing a bit more into your first day, I recommend visiting Vor Frelser Kirke (Our Savior's Church) and enjoying the marvelous view from the top of the Church's tower.

This beautiful cathedral is located next to Christiania and has many intriguing stories behind it. It starts with the declaration of absolute monarchy by King Frederik III after long, bloody wars that led to the loss of the southern parts of Denmark in 1660. His son, Christian V, cemented the declaration of absolute monarchy in Denmark by commissioning the building and consecration of the Our Savior's Church.

The church was built in the 1680s and consecrated in 1696, taking over 14 years for completion. The foundations were laid by covering up and filling up the seabed, which is the reason why the construction time was so long. This baroque style church was Christian V's greatest work and serves as a legacy left behind for his country and his people. Today, Our Savior's Church is not just a large tourist attraction but also a thriving parish for many Danes.

The Tower of Our Savior's Church – The spire or tower were consecrated more than 50 years later in 1752 during the reign of Christian V's son, Christian VI. Today, the tower is a splendid symbol of Danish culture and religion standing tall and proud. The person who can climb this rather treacherous tower will be rewarded with a stunning view of the Copenhagen city.

Climbing the tower was considered a test of manhood and continues to challenge offbeat tourists. The entire spire is made of oak, which can shake quite a bit when the winds are strong enhancing the feeling of fear for the climber. Of course, there are railings providing throughout the right side of the stairs allowing you to be able to grip onto something solid during the rather difficult climb.

However, when you reach the top and touch the gilded globe, you may feel a rush of adrenaline that will quickly melt your fatigue away.

Be aware that the church closes at 3.30 p.m. and the tower closes at 4:00 p.m.

How much time: Set aside at least 1 hour for both the church and climbing the tower.

Extra if More Time: The National Museum of Denmark

If you are a history buff or enjoy museums, I highly recommend a visit to the National Museum of Denmark which is practically located on your way to Vesterbro.

Personally, I don't visit many museums on my city trips as this is not my preference. However, I value the biggest and important ones, and I have visited The National Museum numerous times. It is the largest and most significant cultural and historical museum in Denmark and also regarded as the most important. Thus, a great choice if you were only to visit one museum. The museum has exhibitions from ancient times up to the 20th century.

The permanent exhibitions at the National Museum include:

- The Danish Prehistory

- The Danish Middle Ages and Renaissance

- Stories of Denmark

- The Royal Collection of Coins and Medals

- Classical and Near Eastern Antiquities

- Ethnographic Collections

- The Children's Museum

An extraordinary gem: Klunkehjemmet

The National Museum of Denmark has a special and unique little pearl of a gem that I recommend to everybody the least interested in experiencing an authentic historical setting. That is the tour of Klunkehjemmet. Klunkehjemmet is an apartment in Copenhagen that has been maintained the same for more than 100 years. To me the experience is almost like traveling in time, because you walk into a family's home from that time and get to experience a remarkable apartment while being educated by the guide on how a wealthy family lived 100 years ago. The apartment has not been remodeled or altered as is the case with most exhibitions. It is the actual apartment and furniture that people lived in.

How much time: 1-3 hours

Address: Ny Vestergade 10 / Prinsens Palæ / DK-1471 København K / +45 3313 4411

4. Vesterbro (Neighborhood Strolling)
Free of charge

Another neighborhood not to be missed is Vesterbro, which I recommend next on day 1.

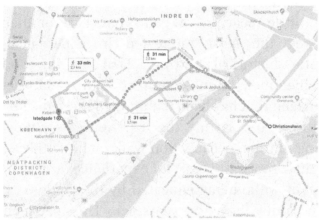

Source: Google Maps

Together with Nørrebro, Vesterbro is considered the hipster neighborhood of Copenhagen. Not many decades ago, Vesterbro was trashy and anything but hot. It was an unmaintained area for drunks, hookers and generally the lower working class. Today the drunks and the hookers are still represented in certain areas, but now they are staying side by side with wealthy inhabitants who can afford to live close to the ultimate center of Copenhagen which is often associated with Rådhuspladsen (City Hall Square). Even the flats on Istedgade, which is considered the roughest area in Vesterbro, are very pricy today.

When strolling Vesterbro, I suggest that you focus in on the area around Istedgade (the end near Copenhagen Central Station) and Kødbyen.

Istedgade

Istedgade is a street that starts out at Copenhagen Central Station and continues through to Enghave Plads all in all around 2 km. Istedgade is however roughly divided into two halves. The end near Enghave Plads away from the city center is relatively quiet and blend in well with the rest of Vesterbro. The end close to the central station, however, represents a different less posh part of Copenhagen with a distinctive atmosphere. This part is famous for being lively and unlike other areas with its sex shops, striptease clubs, prostitutes, pubs, drug addicts, alcoholics and homeless people.

This part of Istedgade is considered the "ruff" part of Copenhagen.

There are many hotels and restaurants in this area. Take a stroll down Istedgade starting at Copenhagen Central Station if you wish to experience a colorful part of

Copenhagen and perhaps stop for dinner at one of the many Asian restaurants in the area.

Kødbyen (The Meatpacking District)

At Vesterbro you also find the meatpacking district (Kødbyen) which is considered one of the hottest areas in town for dining, clubbing and as a general cultural scene.

Kødbyen is probably the most popular area for going out. Besides restaurants, you find art galleries, night clubs and also the butchers that initially did business here are still to be found.

Consider saving your appetite for one of the many gorgeous eateries in Kødbyen.

I have had one of my best pizza experiences at the Italian restaurant called Mother which is located here, and there are many other excellent choices here like Cocks and Cows which might be the best burger joint in town.

Kødbyen is a contemporary must-see, and it represents a modern cultural contrast to the old part of Copenhagen that is highly represented in this itinerary.

For more information on what to see and do in the Meatpacking District:

https://www.visitcopenhagen.com/copenhagen/meatpacking-district

Værnedamsvej

If time allows, while you are at Vesterbro make your way down Værnedamsvej. The street is located a bit further away from the center but worth the detour. This relatively short street offers a variety of iconic shops, bars, and restaurants and has a unique atmosphere you don't find anywhere else at Vesterbro. For this reason, it is probably the most popular street at Vesterbro amongst the locals.

Don't miss: Wine at Falernum

Day 1 Itinerary Map

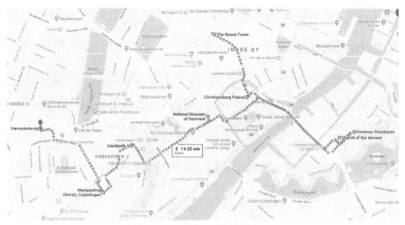

Source: Google Maps

6

Day 2 – More of Central Copenhagen

1. Nyhavn
Free of charge

I recommend starting the day by walking along Nyhavn.

Nyhavn is a scenic waterfront in Copenhagen with plenty of restaurants and its one of the most popular places to visit in Copenhagen. On a pleasant summer day, it will be packed with tourists as well as locals. However, in the morning it is usually not so bad.

Constructed in the 17th century, Nyhavn is considered to be the entertainment and canal district of Copenhagen. There was a time when Nyhavn was a commercial port where ships from all across the world docked. It was a picture replete with sailors, alehouses and, of course, ladies of pleasure.

Modern-day Nyhavn is as beautiful as ever with the old buildings and houses being renovated and converted into restaurants where scents of food and drink and jazz music fill the air. House #9, Nyhavn is considered to be the oldest home in existence from 1681. Its design remains unaltered even to this day. Another exciting aspect of Nyhavn is that many of the houses here have been the homes of leading and famous artists. For example, House #20 is the place where Hans Christian Andersen lived and wrote some of his legendary fairy tales.

Copenhageners absolutely love going to Nyhavn during summer for the holiday-like atmosphere. On a hot summer day expect Nyhavn to be fully packed with people everywhere even sitting on the ground by the water.

A Nyhavn Christmas is famous all over replete with Danish Christmas delicacies served in all the restaurants along with the yearly Christmas market that fills the cobbled streets of the district.

How much time: Depending on the size of the crowd, it takes about 20-25 minutes to walk all the way through Nyhavn which is highly recommended. If you want to have lunch or perhaps coffee, then set aside the extra time.

2. Canal Boat Tour

This is perhaps not technically regarded a must-see sight in Copenhagen. However, the guided tour is a delightful way to experience Copenhagen from the water and get a lot of information and insight about the city, and I feel like I must include it as a "must-do". The Canal Boat Tour starts at Nyhavn and ends there as well, which makes it the perfect next adventure on day 1.

It is no secret that the Copenhageners love to take the tour as well during summer. Personally, I have been going for a tour a handful of times, and a canal tour is one of my favorite summer activities in Copenhagen

I recommend choosing Nettobådende for the guided tour which is the cheaper but still excellent alternative:

How much time: The tour takes about 1 hour from start to end.

Starting points: **Nyhavn** at Heibergsgade and **Holmens Church** opposite the old Stock-Exchange

3. Amalienborg Palace

The second site on day two is Amalienborg Palace – home to the royal family.

Source: Google Maps

Denmark is one of the oldest monarchies in the world. I'll dare to say that Amalienborg Palace is an extremely "Danish" sight, because the monarchy inarguably is a considerable part of the Danish DNA. Experiencing the Royal Guard together with the royal atmosphere at the palace square makes the palace worth a visit.

The palace serves as the residence for the royal family primarily in the winter months. Take notice if a flag is up on one of the four rooftops. This signals that members of the royal family are currently residing inside the walls of the palace.

The Royal Life Guard stand watch at Amalienborg Palace, and the Life Guard is one of the exciting things to experience when visiting Amalienborg Palace. With their very distinctive uniforms and the purpose of protecting the Danish monarchy, many Danes perceive the Royal Life Guide to being something very Danish and great pride to Danes.

The Life Guard is on duty 24 hours a day. Every day at noon the Life Guard has a change of watch ceremony, and it is highly recommended for you to be there at noon to experience this.

The ceremony begins at Rosenborg Palace at 11.30 where the Life Guard march in a group and arrives at Amalienborg Palace at 12. When the Queen resides in the palace, the guard is also accompanied by the Royal Guards music band. This takes place in the winter months between September and April.

Recommended arrival time: Noon

How much time: It will take you about 20-30 min of strolling around to complete a visit to this place. If you wish to follow the guard on their tour from Rosenborg to Amalienborg then add another 30 minutes of walking.

Address: Amalienborg Slotsplads / 1257 København K

Extra if More Time: Marmorkirken (Frederiks Kirke)

Marmorkirken (The Marble Church or Frederik's Church) lies only 150 meters from Amalienborg Palace and is a recommended extra stop after Amalienborg if time allows and you wish for fuller schedule. The official name of the church is Frederik's Church, but among Copenhageners, it is more popularly known as "the Marble Church" which is connected with its most prominent feature.

The Marble Church is one of the most magnificent churches in the city with its impressive large copper dome and beautiful breath-taking interior. There are services in Danish every Sunday and Holidays at 10.30, and the church is also a prevalent church to get married. In those occasions and in case of concerts the church will not be accessible. However, every Saturday and Sunday as well as every day between June 15 and August 31, there are visits to the dome at 1 pm.

Recommended arrival time: 1 pm (for dome visit)

How much time: 1-2 hours

Address: Frederiksgade 4, 1265 København

Extra if More Time: Langelinie: The Little Mermaid and Kastellet

Free of charge

Langelinie is a long path right by the harbor that offers stunning scenery for walking on a beautiful summer's day. It also happens to be the home of the Little Mermaid.

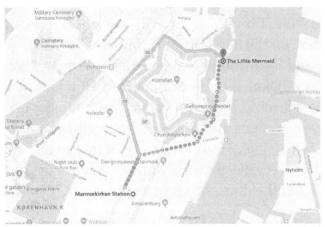

Source: Google Maps

The Little Mermaid

A lot can be said about this little icon. Copenhageners for sure have mixed opinions on the statuette. There seems to be a general consensus that she is highly overrated at least as an attraction, and I agree with that. I'm sure most guide books will find her a must-see and important, and God knows that many tourists flock around her every summer.

The Little Mermaid is little indeed. Locals, in general, find it funny that this small sculpture can attract such a crazy number of tourists year after year, however, we do recognize the importance of the story and symbolic of our beloved mermaid. Inspired by the fairy tale of the same name written by Danish author, Hans Christian Andersen, the statue is made of granite and bronze, and it was gifted by Carl Jacobsen, the famous Carlsberg Brewery owner.

The mermaid gives up everything she believed in for the sake of her beloved, a handsome, young prince of the land. The statue reflects the yearning of the mermaid as she swims up from her deep-sea home every morning and perches herself on the rock, waiting patiently and longingly for a little glimpse of her beloved prince. I'm sure you are also familiar with the Disney movie based on this fairytale.

The sculptor who made this statue was Edvard Eriksen.

How much time: Set aside half an hour to an hour if you wish to stroll along the harbor. Otherwise the Little Mermaid can be experienced in just a few minutes.

Address: Langelinie, 2100 København Ø

Kastellet

If time allows, consider going for a walk around Kastellet which is located very close to the Little Mermaid. This star-shaped fortress was commissioned initially by Frederic III. Today, it stands as proof of the beauty of Danish architecture and sense of style that has not ebbed even in modern times. Replete with a splendid moat that surrounds the fortress and grassy verdant ramparts, Kastellet boasts a beautiful chapel and a historic windmill.

How much time: It will take you about 30-60 min of strolling around to complete a visit to the fortress.

Address: Gl. Hovedvagt, Kastellet 1, 2100 København

4. Rosenborg Castle and Kongens have

To get from Amalienborg (or Langelinie) to Rosenborg Castle, you need to do a bit of walking and/or go by public transportation as it is located about 2 km apart.

Source: Google Maps

Rosenborg Castle

Built by one of the important Danish kings, Christian IV, the Rosenborg Castle houses not only the crown jewels of the royal family but also hundreds of years of history within its ramparts. Kings and queens have lived in the castle which today serves as a museum. The castle is a must-see because of its historical and cultural importance regarding the Danish monarchy and because the crown jewels are quite simply breathtaking.

How much time: It will take you about 1-2 hours of strolling around to complete a visit to this place.

Address: Øster Voldgade 4A, 1350 København

Kongens have

Rosenborg Castle is placed inside the beautiful park Kongens Have which in English means the king's garden. Kongens Have is perfect for a picnic or a stroll if weather permits. It is one of the Danes favorite parks in Copenhagen not least because of the location and the very open scenery with fields of grass for picnic and play.

Day 2 Itinerary Map

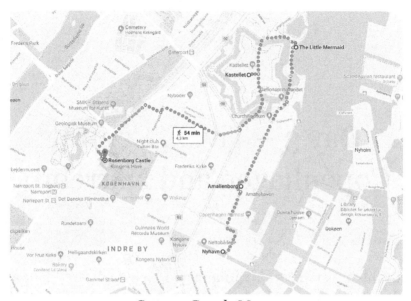

Source: Google Maps

7

Day 3 – Tivoli, Central Copenhagen and Nørrebro

In this must-see 3-day itinerary, I have dedicated half a day for a visit to Tivoli Gardens. The second part of the day is for exploring more of the Copenhagen city center, Rådhuspladsen, and Strøget as well as Nørrebro and the lakes.

1. Tivoli Gardens

Yes, it does cost a bit of money, but I will dare to say that a visit to Copenhagen is not really full without going to

Tivoli. In addition to the games and fun rides, Tivoli Gardens is unique to Copenhagen considering the fact that this place is what inspired Walt Disney to build Disneyworld and Michael Jackson was so impressed with it that he was planning to buy it for himself!

The theme park itself with its fun rides and games is extremely lively in summer. Even in the winter, there is a lovely coziness about the theme park here. Of course, the food stalls, the fabulous exhibitions, and the amazingly well-maintained gardens enhance the wonderment of the place even further.

It is easy to get lost in Tivoli Gardens and lose track of time and, therefore, it makes sense to dedicate many hours to this place.

Things to do in Tivoli Gardens

Tivoli Gardens is not just an amusement park (it is one of the oldest ones – opened way back in 1843); it is much more than that. Again, many of the rides are scintillating actually. However, the atmosphere in the garden is charming. Replete with quaint walkways, adrenaline-pumping rides, not-so-scary rides for the entire family, a variety of restaurants, and millions (actually eight hundred thousand) of lights (magical scene if you choose to stay late into the evening), Tivoli Gardens is a must-visit for any tourist with or without kids in tow.

There are two halls within the gardens, the Tivoli Concert Hall and the Glass Hall, both of which host a multitude of spellbinding shows. So, what can you do in Tivoli Gardens? Well, let me start with the most obvious.

Thrilling Rides – With names like Demon, the Aquila, the Astronomer and more, there are rides that will turn you upside down, take you on journeys to outer space, and scare you to bits, every one of the thrilling rides in Tivoli Gardens will induce adrenaline leaving the memories embedded for a long time.

Family Rides – For the kids and those family members who are terrified of 'thrills,' there are some amazing smile-inducing rides including The Little Dragon, The Dragon Boats, The Classic Carousel, The Lighthouse, and more. These rides are bound to bring a happy smile onto everyone's faces.

I have named only a few rides. There are many, many more for you to try out. You could first walk around, make a note of the ones you want to try out, and then take the next couple of hours walking round to try out the rides.

Entertainment – Events and entertainment galore here! Every week, the organizers plan for fun events aligned with the particular ongoing season such as outdoor concerts in the summer and Christmas wonderland in winter.

Every Saturday in the summer season there is a firework show beginning at 2345 hours.

Food and Drinks – With over 40 restaurants and cafes, Tivoli Gardens has the largest selection of eating places in the whole of Copenhagen. Ranging from gourmet food to the best available street food varieties, you can try all the cuisine including traditional Danish cuisine in this one place.

The Gardens – The rides, the restaurants, the history, and all other elements are scattered across the verdant Tivoli Gardens where you can simply stroll around and feast your eyes and other senses on the enchanting beauty of one of the oldest amusement parks in the world.

The Tivoli Youth Guard – An interesting piece of history is right here in the Tivoli Gardens. There are 100 children, referred to as the Lilliputian Military, a tradition that dates back to 1844, when Georg Carstensen, the founder, set up this music band as a gift to the garden for its second season. The Tivoli Youth Guard is still alive, kicking, and creating fantastic band music for all visitors.

Opening Hours and Seasons

Note that Tivoli is *not* open all year.

There are three seasons when Tivoli Gardens is open to the public; summer, Halloween, and Christmas. Summer season begins around the end of March and goes on until the end of September. The Halloween season starts mid-October and goes on until the first week of November and the Christmas season starts of mid-November and goes on until 31 December. Sunday-Thursday it opens at 1100 hours and closes at 2300 hours. Fridays and Saturdays, it closes at 2400 hours.

You have to buy entry tickets which have different prices for adults and children. There are annual cards and other kinds of cards as well which come with their own set of discounts and deals. You can check out https://www.tivoligardens.com/ for more details.

Recommended arrival time: Arrive as early as possible for the least number of visitors and to avoid standing in long lines.

How much time: You can easily spend half a day and upwards a whole day in Tivoli.

Address: Vesterbrogade 3, 1630 København V

2. Rådhuspladsen
Free of charge

Next up Rådhuspladsen which is located right next to Tivoli.

Source: Google Maps

This is the central square of Copenhagen in front of City Hall and considered the absolute center of Copenhagen. It buzzes with action that many times borders on chaos, especially during the summer. However, the charm of this place is in its noise and chaos, and it's great for people watching. Life is brimming at Rådhuspladsen.

Rådhuspladsen is special to the Copenhageners. This is where the national sports teams are celebrated when they return home from World Cup victories and other great accomplishments. On New Year's Eve, the square is packed with locals around midnight. The tower is very famous among the Danes for its Town Hall Bells and the clock which is broadcasted live on national TV just before 12 o'clock on New Year's Eve.

Rådhuspladsen is a must-visit to revel in the noise and chaos that is central to this central location of the city.

Moreover, Rådhuspladsen is the connecting point to Strøget, the central shopping street in the city.

3. Strøget (The Pedestrian Street)
Free of charge

Start walking down Strøget from Rådhuspladsen.

Source: Google Maps

This pedestrian street is the longest walking street in Europe, and you will have plenty of opportunities to do some power shopping here. It's busy all year round and beggars, backgammon players, dice players, and street musicians try to make a living here and there. A heads up;

this is a very touristy part of Copenhagen and so much so that local Copenhageners often won't be bothered to walk down Strøget. However, it is an exciting street to walk for newcomers. Try also to explore the side streets, you might just find a hidden gem in the form of a cute boutique or a lovely café.

Extra if More Time: The Black Diamond – The Royal Danish Library

This contemporary building stands out amidst the beauty of the 'old' Copenhagen creating that seamlessness of the old with the new. While book lovers might be beckoned in, for others, the mere sight of the modern building is sufficient to delight. In fact, you don't need to go visit the Black Diamond to get a good view. If you go on the canal tour, you can see and enjoy it in all its exterior marvel. This library also houses the National Museum of Photography, which is also worth a visit, if time permits.

How much time: Less than 1 hour

Address: Søren Kierkegaards Plads 1, 1221 København K

4. Nørrebro and the Lakes (Neighborhood walking)

Nørrebro

From Strøget head to Nørreport Station and walk further on to the neighborhood called Nørrebro (København N).

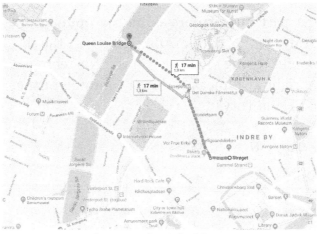

Source: Google Maps

Nørrebro could be categorized as particularly hipster and artsy, and it is one of the more multicultural parts of Copenhagen. Nørrebro seems unpredictable and has a great variety of trendy bars, designer shops as well as bodegas.

While walking to Nørrebro from the city center make sure to cross the bridge called Dronning Louise's Bro (The Bridge of Queen Louise). This bridge is iconic amongst locals especially the younger crowd who love to hang out on the bridge in the summer while sipping beer and sometimes listening to music.

The first part of Nørrebro is, in my opinion, the most interesting for a stroll. After crossing the bridge, I recommend going further down Nørrebrogade and turning right at Elmegade. Then continue further down to Sankt Hans Torv.

The Lakes

If time permits, consider a stroll around one or more of the 3 lakes – altogether 5 basins divided by bridges. The lakes are among the Copenhagener's favorite walks.

One of the appealing aspects of Copenhagen is the fact that it is surrounded by large areas of greenery and water. The nearness to the sea gives the city its rich plethora of harbors and docks and canals too. In addition to these, there are the lakes in Copenhagen which together are referred to as 'Søerne' including Sortedams Sø, Peblinge Sø, and Sankt Jørgens Sø.

Today, the lakes are used primarily for leisure and recreational purposes where the locals hang out together. Like Islands Brygge and its Harbor Bath, these lakes are frequented by local families during weekends. You can see them relaxing under the sun or picnicking in the verdant surroundings. The lakes are unfit for swimming and jumping into the water is not allowed.

There are walking paths and biking paths all around the lakes, and they are very suitable for a peaceful walk but also to mingle with and know more about the Danish culture from the locals.

Extra if More Time: Night-stroll at Amager Strandpark

Amager Strandpark is a large man-made beach park with lots of space and long walking paths. The beach park is very popular amongst the Copenhageners. It's located not far from the airport and only 5 metro stops (Øresund station) from Nørreport station.

Going for a stroll along the beach path is highly recommended after a long day in the vibrant city. In the summer evenings, groups of young Danes often gather to have a bonfire and listen to music on the beach which creates an extraordinary atmosphere. That is definitely modern hygge in action.

The beach park is obviously also suitable for a day-time visit.

Day 3 Itinerary Map

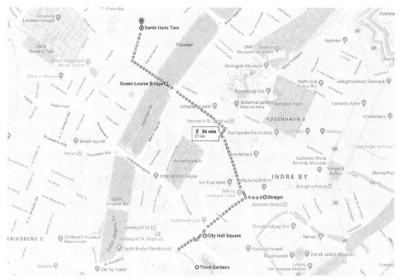

Source: Google Maps

8

The 3-Day-Must-See Itinerary - Overview

So, I have been taking you through my greatest version of a 3-day itinerary in Copenhagen. I hope you got wildly inspired and now have a relatively good idea of how to spend your days in the city.

For the sake of simplicity, I will list all the sights and activities in chronological order here, so you can quickly look up the full itinerary.

I will end this chapter with what I like to call the Ultimate Prioritization, which consists of the top three sights that I would recommend you prioritize above all else on a short trip. These are such distinctive landmarks when it comes to Copenhagen. They are not "just" statues (nothing wrong with statues though!) but three remarkable areas where you can interact and get an intimate feel of this city.

Day 1:

1. Rundetårn

2. Christiansborg

3. Christiania and Christianshavn neighborhood walk

Extra: Our Savior's Church

Extra: The National Museum

4. Vesterbro neighborhood walk

Day 2:

1. Nyhavn

2. Canal Tour

3. Amalienborg Palace

Extra: Marmorkirken

Extra: The Little Mermaid

Extra: Kastellet

4. Rosenborg Castle and Kongens Have

Day 3:

1. Tivoli Gardens

2. Rådhuspladsen

3. Strøget

Extra: The Black Diamond

4. Nørrebro and The Lakes neighborhood walk

Extra: Night stroll at Amager Beach Park

The Ultimate Prioritization

If your stay is less than 3 days or you just can't make all of the above then the three most remarkable must-see sites in Copenhagen, that I would prioritize above all else, include:

1. Tivoli Garden
2. Christiania
3. Nyhavn

+ if the weather allows and you have an extra hour when at Nyhavn go by the **Canal tour**. You will get an extensive Copenhagen experience and a lot of understanding about the city in a short amount of time.

9

What to Add if More Than 3 Days

Now, if you plan a 4-, 5- or a 6-day trip, the following places can easily fit into your itinerary. I would also characterize these sights as must-sees, but they will fit better if you are lucky enough to have more than 3 days for your Copenhagen adventure as they are either located outside Copenhagen or further away from the city center.

Day 4 – Kronborg Castle and Louisiana

For day 4 I recommend going a bit outside of the city for two major attractions that are located just north of Copenhagen. These are widely famous for good reason and maybe you have already heard of them:

- Kronborg Castle
- Louisiana Museum of Modern Art

Kronborg Castle

Referred to as Kronborg Slot in Danish, this castle is a UNESCO World Heritage Site. This Renaissance castle played a significant role in the history of Denmark. With impressive architecture, Kronborg Castle's present structure is a result of multiple expansions and reconstructions that took place throughout the 16th and the 17th centuries on an older castle that is known to have been in existence since 1420.

Kronborg Castle, located in Helsingør north of Copenhagen, held a very strategic position in history. It controlled a water passage between Denmark and Sweden, an important trade outlet into the Baltic Sea. Along with Karnan Castle on the Sweden side, Kronborg controlled and stood guard over the important sea outlet.

Another matter of interest about Kronborg Castle is the fact that Shakespeare chose to set his play, Hamlet, here.

There are restaurants and cafes within the castle to keep you fed and happy while you tour the castle. There is free Wi-Fi available which will help you get fascinating anecdotes about the various rooms and artifacts all over the castle.

If you are traveling with elderly people or those with compromised walking abilities, you must know that buggies and wheelchairs are available but only for access to the Courtyard. Indoor tours are walking tours only.

There are group tours organized by the authorities that you can choose, or you can simply walk around the castle on your own, learning and experience the lives of the kings and queens from the past.

How much time: You can easily spend half a day or more at Kronborg Castle

Address: Kronborg 2 C, 3000 Helsingør.

Louisiana Museum of Modern Art

An absolute must-see for the art lover, the Louisiana Museum of Modern Art, located in Humlebæk town, north of Copenhagen, is a haven for modern and contemporary art. With a vast collection of over 3500 artwork pieces, this museum holds exhibitions several times during the year dedicated to various art forms.

Louisiana is primarily famous for artwork and paintings from the end of WWII until today. In addition, it promotes and tracks the movement of Danish architecture. The purpose of setting up the Louisiana Museum of Modern Art in 1958 was to collect and protect all of Danish modern art.

After it achieved an impressive collection of Danish art, the museum started focusing on the contemporary and modern art collections of other countries as well. The museum picked out beautiful art objects, paintings, sculptures, and artifacts selectively and brought them to the Louisiana Museum.

For any art lover, whether novice or experienced, the Louisiana Museum of Modern Art should be included without an iota of doubt. It holds the record of the most visited museum in the entire country. In addition to feasting your eyes, heart, and mind on the fabulous art collection, you could enjoy yourself in the spacious surroundings outside the museum that is filled with sculptures, statues, beautiful sloping terrains, and a very well-maintained garden.

Recommended arrival time: In weekends especially on rainy days Louisiana is packed with visitors. Try to visit on weekdays within working hours and/or if possible when the weather is nice.

How much time: You can easily spend upwards to 3 hours in this place. For hardcore art lovers, you might even want to dedicate more time here.

Address: Gl. Strandvej 13, 3050 Humlebæk.

Day 5 – Calsberg Brewery and Copenhagen Zoo

Carlsberg Brewery

Back in Copenhagen on day 5, Carlsberg Brewery offers an exclusive experience around the premises. Perfect for beer lovers and even if you are not, still perfect for summer outings, Carlsberg Brewery is a frequently visited tourist hotspot in Copenhagen. At the Carlsberg Brewery, you will be subjected to the most exquisite sensations associated with beer.

- You can smell the ingredients
- You can see the beauty of the authentic architecture
- You can taste the famous Danish beer in varying styles and flavors
- You can meet the brewer horses

There are some fascinating sights within the Carlsberg Brewery precincts:

There is an enormous collection of beer bottles here; it is considered to be the most extensive beer collection in the whole world.

You can see the entire history of beer brewing in one small compact room. Small as it may be, this room contains everything you need to know about beer brewing and its history and the evolution of the beer brewing process

A small sculpture garden contains some personal art pieces belonging to Carl Jacobsen, the son of the founder of the brewery. There is a replica of the Little Mermaid statue, the original of which is at another famous tourist attraction in Copenhagen. The original was donated to the city by Carl Jacobsen himself!

Then comes the brewery stables with its collection of draft horses; another fascinating thing to see here.

The summer ticket can include a horse carriage ride. You will be taken on a scenic journey around the town of old Carlsberg which sprung up after the brewery was built.

Visiting the Carlsberg Brewery is terrific because you get to see Copenhagen beyond its palaces and the bustling city center.

How much time: 1-3 hours

Address: Valby Langgade 1, 2500 København.

Note: Carlsberg Visitor Center is closed in all of 2019 due to renovation and modernization. It opens again for the public in 2020.

Copenhagen Zoo

In the same neighborhood as Carlsberg Brewery, only a 10-minute walk through Søndermarken lies Copenhagen Zoo which makes for a great next visit on day 5. The Zoo lies on top of the hill "Valby Bakke" with the distinct Zoo tower right by the entrance.

Copenhagen Zoo is one of the oldest in Europe and among other things it has a famous elephant house which can also be seen from outside the Zoo in Frederiksberg Have.

The Zoo houses in its 11 acres more than 4000 animals and 230 different species and also has a large dedicated area for children.

A recently added attraction worth noticing is the two adorable pandas that Copenhagen borrowed from China in April 2019. The Zoo has built entirely new areas for the pandas to live in for the next 15 years.

A day-pass costs around 180-195 DKK for adults and 100 DKK for children.

How much time: Set aside 3 hours for a full visit including lunch

Address: Roskildevej 32, 2000 Frederiksberg.

Extra if More Time: Frederiksberg Have and The Cisterns

If time allows, consider going for a stroll in *Frederiksberg Have* which is a park right next to the Zoo or visit the remarkable underground *Cisterns* right across the street from the Zoo in Søndermarken.

Day 6 - Dyrehaven

Dyrehaven and Dyrehavsbakken (Bakken)

The second oldest amusement park is the Tivoli Gardens, which we covered on day 3 of the must-see itinerary. The oldest one and lesser famous is just north of Copenhagen. It is called "Dyrehavsbakken" or just in short "Bakken". Bakken is built at the entrance of a vast wooded area or park called Dyrehaven (Deer Park).

You will need to take a train to get to Dyrehaven, and it takes about 30 minutes from Copenhagen Central Station.

As the name suggests, this park is a haven for deer, and if your luck holds, you will find herds of them (red and fallow) grazing in peaceful splendor as you walk through the myriad of paths that meander in this serene place. However, no guarantees implied. You may not get to see even a single deer. But, the offbeat traveler in you will be happy for finding this fabulous and semi-hidden location right outside Copenhagen.

How much time: Set aside at least 3 hours for a full visit including lunch

Address: Dyrehavevej 62, 2930 Klampenborg.

Extra if More Time: Bellevue Beach

Outside of Dyrehaven next to the train station Klampenborg you will find Bellevue Beach, a trendy beach among the locals. This beach is lovely and quite packed with sunbathing visitors and beach volley players on a hot summer day. Remember to pack your bathing suit!

10

Traveling with Kids

Traveling with kids creates other challenges as compared to traveling alone or in the company of adults. What does Copenhagen have for children? Children hold a special place for the people of Copenhagen. Ranging from reserved seats in public transport to dedicated playgrounds spread across the city to kid-friendly hotels and restaurants, the city of Copenhagen ensures that kids are treated with the dignity and respect and love each of them deserves. While some of these are repetitions from the must-see itinerary, here is a collection the top things you can include for kids during your visit to Copenhagen:

Tivoli

If traveling with kids, Tivoli should be a no-brainer. It is perhaps the most exciting place for a child to spend a day, even the former and quite child-like Michael Jackson fell madly in love with this huge and magnificent "playground" that he wanted to buy it as I have mentioned.

Children of all ages are excited and quite possibly want to pull away from their parents to go on different rides. All over the park, the happy screaming is unmistakable, and the atmosphere will leave most feeling uplifted. Tivoli has plenty of eateries, bars, shopping, and rides and with children, you can easily spend a whole day.

Address: Vesterbrogade 3, 1630 København V.

Experimentarium

Suitable for children of all ages, there are plenty of games and activities to keep them engaged for several hours. These exciting activities include liquids sputtering and fizzing, the air filling with soap bubbles, and more. Children can explore and learn about science, math, and technology in a highly engaged and fun way. Some of the things you and your kids can do here are:

- Tunnel of Senses – where you can experience all the senses
- Labyrinth of Light – where you will be tricked and amazed by the effects of light and darkness
- Interactive Film Theater – where you can be part of a film
- 16 interactive and engaging exhibitions and activities spread across two floors

Experimentarium is mainly an indoor facility and very suitable for those rainy days.

Address: Tuborg Havnevej 7, 2900 Hellerup

Dyrehavsbakken (Bakken)

Set amidst Dyrehaven a green park that boasts really ancient trees (some of them over 400 years old) and home to over 2000 deer, Bakken is the oldest amusement park in the world. You can spend half the day in the lush green surroundings of the deer park where you have ample space and greenery for a picnic and playing around and spend the remaining part of the day in the amusement park in the fun rides available in plenty.

Address: Dyrehavevej 62, 2930 Klampenborg

Den Blå Planet

This is the National Aquarium of Denmark. Built to give visitors, both kids and adults, an immersive experience of the ocean world, this building has five arms of over four million liters of seawater that hold multiple varieties of exotic sea and ocean creatures that could leave your kids (and you) spellbound.

You will be able to see hammerhead sharks swimming with moray eels and ray fish, the water animals of the Coral Reef, and piranhas and anacondas too. There is a dedicated space for land creatures as well where you can see animals from the Amazon including birds and butterflies flying around. Don't miss this place if you are traveling with kids.

Address: Jacob Fortlingsvej 1, 2770 Kastrup

Tycho Brahe Planetarium

With a Space Theater right in the middle of the planetarium, you and your kids can experience the joys of space travel and astronomy. The highly immersive activities include getting lost in the starry sky, 3D and IMAX movies that will take you right into space, and the permanent exhibition regales you with stories of space travels and astronomy. Moreover, both you and your kids will come away more knowledgeable about our planet and this vast universe than when you entered the planetarium.

Address: Gl. Kongevej 10, 1610 København V

Copenhagen Zoo

A place loved by kids, Copenhagen Zoo has a variety of exotic animals including polar bears, monkeys, lions, hippos, elephants and more. The Zoo holds over 4000 animals from as many as 264 species. There is a separate section in the Copenhagen Zoo called the Children's Zoo. Here you can meet farm animals and pat and touch African dwarf goats. Here, you can also see horses being trained and pat them while they eat their lunch.

Moreover, the elephant facility is considered to be one of the topmost of the world. Here, you can see and experience the elephants at very close quarters. You can watch them bathing in a special water bath that is deep enough to cover these large animals completely.

The Arctic Ring in the Copenhagen Zoo houses polar bears in addition to seals and other North Atlantic animals and birds. In recent addition, the Zoo now holds two pandas borrowed from China.

Address: Roskildevej 32, 2000 Frederiksberg

Louisiana Children's Wing

There is a children's wing in the Louisiana Museum of Modern Art where you and your kids can have a frolicking time by participating in various activities held here. The features of the Children's Wing include a Story-Telling Room, a Computer Room, and select Sunday workshops for both kids and their parents.

Address: Gl. Strandvej 13, 3050 Humlebæk

The Zoological Museum

Here, you and your kids can watch the process of evolution as proposed by Darwin through a permanent (and the biggest in the world) exhibition that documents and brings alive his ideas of evolution through a variety of fossils, skeletons, and animals. This evolution exhibition continues even after the point where Darwin's theory ends and brings you to the present day! There is a room referred to as the National History Laboratory where you can touch and feel stuffed skeletons and animals.

Address: Universitetsparken 15, 2100 København

III

Staying and Thriving in Copenhagen

"Our happiest moments as tourists always seem to come when we stumble upon one thing while in pursuit of something else."

- Lawrence Block

This part covers the general aspects of accommodation, transportation including areas in Copenhagen, shopping, transportation tips, the best of dining and other Danish tips for thriving through your 3-day vacation in Copenhagen. Towards the end, I will include some inside information about what locals love in Copenhagen and what those Danes like as well as how you could easily connect with them should you wish so.

11

Accommodation

If you have already booked accommodation, you could skip this part, as I will be covering where to stay. However, you might find the neighborhood characteristics an interesting read, so maybe just stay tuned.

I expect that your choice of accommodation somewhat depends on both your budget and preference and because that is individual, I will not cover the subject of choosing accommodation-type. Instead, I will give you pointers regarding the choice of location. I always find that particularly for a short trip, the choice of location is important for two reasons; First, it is obviously time-saving to live in an area close to the attractions you want to experience. Secondly, I find that neighborhood-strolling is a significant part of the city experience, and you might as well stay in a charming neighborhood where you want to be strolling as you will be walking around your place anyway. Thus, if possible, choose your accommodation in a fascinating area that captures some of the uniqueness of the city that you would like to experience.

Neighborhood Characteristics

Here I have listed the particular Copenhagen neighborhoods I would recommend if you want a prime location as a tourist. Further down, I have included other options as well that are in a reasonable distance from Rådhuspladsen (which is considered the very center of Copenhagen) and with good transportation facilities.

København K

As you undoubtedly have noticed in the previous part of this book, many of the must-see attractions are located in the city center called København K. On top of that, København K is a very historical area with many old buildings and remarkable architecture. I find this neighborhood to be incredibly atmospherically, historical as well as internationally urban. Besides the sightseeing monuments, it offers shopping, cafés, restaurants, history, architecture, parks and waterfronts. I find that there is always something interesting to look at, and I always enjoy strolling around this neighborhood. It's great for people watching, and there are many shops close by almost wherever you are in this neighborhood. The area around Amalienborg has the least amount of shops but then offers an amazing scenic harbor and a majestic atmosphere.

Fun Fact:

In case you are wondering, the "K" that comes after København simply stands for "København". The area is in fact called "København København". In theory, it could as well have been called København C ("C" being short for "center") because it is the center of Copenhagen, but that was not the case.

Christianshavn

I have included at stroll around Christianshavn in the must-see itinerary. Besides being located very close to the city center, Christianshavn has a unique atmosphere and a scenic waterfront, which makes it an excellent location for your stay. At the moment, Christianshavn is the most expensive part of Copenhagen regarding apartment prices, which is a direct result of its popularity. Christianshavn is, in fact, a small individual island, which you don't easily realize since it is very closely connected to København K and Amager.

Christiania and the iconic church Vor Frelser Kirke are both located on Christianshavn. The neighborhood inspires walks by the harbor and around the canals and of course at Christiania. If you want to visit the new street food market Reffen, it will be a 30 minutes' walk from Christianshavn.

København V (Vesterbro)

København V is one of the two hipster neighborhood (København N being the other) and offers a great variety of restaurants and cafés.

The "V" stands for Vesterbro which is the name popularly used for this neighborhood. Vesterbro is a former working-class area turned hip and modern, but it's still somewhat of a center for hookers, drunks, drug addicts and homeless people particularly in certain areas at and around Istedgade. The tourist hotspots of Vesterbro include Kødbyen (the Meatpacking District) and the Carlsberg Brewery. Vesterbro borders København K and the main street called Vesterbrogade starts at Rådhuspladsen.

København N (Nørrebro)

The "N" stands for Nørrebro which is the name popularly used for this neighborhood. This casual, colorful, and young-at-heart neighborhood is a melting pot of multiple cultures, and Nørrebro is the other hipster neighborhood of Copenhagen. The square Sankt Hans Torv is the center of this charming neighborhood and the bridge connecting Nørrebro to København K called "Dronning Louise's bro" is a favorite hangout in summer among locals. The bridge is the start of the lively Nørrebrogade which is the main road where you won't have to look far for pubs or shawarmas. The large cemetery Assistentens Kirkegård which holds the grave of Hans Christian Anderson is located in the middle of Nørrebro. The area around Nørrebrogade close to the lakes is a superb location if you want to stay in a lively area with a multicultural young and hipster atmosphere close to the city center.

Other areas:

Østerbro – Known for the most famous statue of Copenhagen, The Little Mermaid, Østerbro is characterized by wide boulevards, beautiful design and delicacy shops. It is a desireable residential locality in the northern part of Copenhagen bordering København K and Nørrebro.

Amager – With an identity of its own of being an island community, Amager is a beautiful and very varied part of Copenhagen with the beaches lending their splendor to this well-loved neighborhood. Islands Brygge is located very close to Rådhuspladsen and perhaps the best area to stay for a short trip. Amager also holds Copenhagen Airport which is located 9 km from Rådhuspladsen

Frederiksberg – The bourgeois neighborhood of Copenhagen. Also, a very attractive residential locality which is generally associated with traditional values and materialism. It is a high scale and quiet neighborhood and a favorite amongst families who wants to live in a classy and quiet area yet still in the middle of Copenhagen. Frederiksberg is technically not Copenhagen since it is a municipality of its own. However, it is located within Copenhagen. The Vatican state of Denmark you might say.

Valby - Valby is a bit further out than the rest of the neighborhoods mentioned in this list up. However, by train from Valby Station, you can still reach Copenhagen Central Station in only 7 minutes. Valby has a lovely cozy vibe and is mainly residential. If you choose to stay in Valby or any other town further out, I highly recommend that you stay as close to a train station as possible.

12

Transportation

The roads and related infrastructure are very well maintained in Copenhagen. Traveling across the city is easy and convenient. Depending on your physical strength and personal preferences, you can travel by bike, bus, metro trains, or even walk. Bear in mind, that Copenhagen is a relatively small capital but still big enough that you wouldn't be able to rely solely on walking.

Getting from the Airport

From the airport, you have various options to get to your hotel/hostel/Airbnb. You absolutely don't have to take a taxi; this would be a costly option. Public transportation can take you basically everywhere in the city, and it's easy and fast to get from the airport to the city center. You can go by either the metro (subway) or train. Both take less than 20 minutes to reach the city center.

I highly recommend using the website https://www.rejseplanen.dk to get the itinerary to your hotel. I will be talking more about this site further down below.

Copenhagen has a zone system which is not the easiest to understand initially. The city center is mainly located in zone 1. The airport is in zone 4. You will have to buy a three-zone ticket to get from the airport to the city center as you will be traveling through the zones 4-3-1. However, I do not recommend you rely on buying single tickets as that will inevitably be very expensive for three days.

You can get a City Pass which gives you unlimited access to public transport including land and water buses, and metro until the expiry of the pass. A City Pass Small covers the zones 1-4 which will be sufficient if you are not planning on going outside of Copenhagen. The price is currently 200 DKR. for 72 hours for one person unlimited. There are also options to buy 24, 48, 96 and 120 hours. I highly recommend you buy this already at the airport. If you are planning on renting a bike and mainly bike around the city, then the City Pass might be unnecessary. Then buying a single ticket from the airport is a better solution. The price is currently 36 DKR. from the airport to the center (3 zones).

As an alternative to the City Pass, the Copenhagen Card might save you money. You can buy this card online or from your hotel or at certain designated spots spread across the city. Its features include:

- Free admissions to multiple tourist attractions
- A few discounts as well
- Free transport throughout the Copenhagen area

The Copenhagen Card not only saves you money but also time and effort as you will not need to wait in queues to buy tickets and entry passes for every journey and tourist spots.

For more information on the Copenhagen Card visit: https://copenhagencard.com/

For more information on public transportation, the zone system and prices visit: https://dinoffentligetransport.dk

Renting a car

Simply put, I would not recommend renting a car unless you are planning to go outside Copenhagen. It's simply not necessary with a car in Copenhagen, in fact, quite the opposite. Finding parking is such a hassle and expensive. Moreover, many streets in the center are one-way, which makes it rather tricky to get around.

Public Transportation in Copenhagen

It is dependable, punctual, and is connected to almost all nooks and crannies of the city. The choice of transportation depends on where you are going. Buses cover large parts of Copenhagen and might be the better choice in many cases. The metro doesn't yet cover large parts of Copenhagen as there are only two lines. It is currently being expanded though, and the new city ring will be up and running late 2019 or early 2020.

Buses – The A-buses are the primary type of buses in the city and work at 3-7-minute frequencies during rush hours. A-buses are available throughout the day. The rush hours in Copenhagen are between 0700 and 0900 hours in the morning and 1530 and 1730 in the evening. Outside of the rush hours, A-buses work at 10-minute frequencies on average.

The S-buses are the second type of buses in Copenhagen and work at a 5-10-minute frequency during rush hours and at 20-minute frequencies outside the rush hours. There are fewer stops in the journey of an S-bus as compared to that of an A-bus running the same route making the S-bus a faster way to get to your destination than the A-bus. The S-buses operate between 0600 hours and 0100 hours.

The N-buses are the night service buses that operate between 0100 and 0500 hours. The bus stops are easily recognizable because of their signature gray color signs.

Metro – Metro trains work 24 hours and 365 days at 2-3-minute frequencies during rush hours and 3-6-minute frequencies outside rush hours.

Trains – There are different types of trains that operate in such a way that you can travel anytime between 0500 to 0030 hours. There are different frequencies at different times for each type of train. Trains operate outside of Copenhagen as well.

https://rejseplanen.dk_- The website I always use for getting anywhere in Copenhagen.

I absolutely recommend that you use that site when you have access to wi-fi. You simply type in where you are and where you are going, and it shows you the quickest options by public transportation.

So, getting around Copenhagen is not just easy but can be pleasurable as well considering that all important neighborhoods are so close to the city center backed by a reliable and accessible public transport system.

Important: Always travel with a ticket!

Even though you can actually enter the metro, trains and some buses without having to show a ticket, it is absolutely imperative that all travelers have a valid ticket *before* they board the bus, metro, or train. There are strict penalties in the form of big fines if you or any of your family members are caught traveling ticketless. Currently, the fee is 750 DKR. ($ 115 US) per person.

Cycling

In Copenhagen, there are dedicated cycling lanes for added safety and convenience of cyclists.

When cycling in Copenhagen, there are a few official and unofficial rules that would be beneficial to acquaint yourself with as the Copenhageners take these very seriously!

Firstly, there are dedicated cycle lanes at almost every main road, and these lanes are unnoticeably divided into two halves. The half closest to the sidewalk is for "slow" cyclists, and if you are riding in a slow/average speed it is imperative that you stay close to the sidewalk. Fast cyclists want to be able to speed and pass by you easily. I'm not kidding, this is being taken very seriously. The main reason for this is that in Denmark, people use bikes as their primary transportation form when getting to and from work, meeting, basically anything. Thus, people in a hurry need to be able to move quickly just like cars on a highway that have dedicated lanes for speeding.

Secondly, when riding on a cycling lane and you pass a bus stop where a bus has stopped for passengers, you have to stop and let the passengers on and off the bus before you can continue. Unless there is a path where the passengers can walk on to from the bus. This is an official rule and is taking very seriously as well for the safety of the passengers.

Lastly and also an important one; always remember to signal when you need to stop or turn.

13

Shopping

Shopping Areas

There are some fantastic shopping options in Copenhagen and here is a list of the popular choices in the city:

Streets:

Strøget – With shops ranging from the budget-friendly right up to the swanky and expensive global brands, Strøget is one of the longest pedestrian shopping areas in all of Europe. It is a must-visit at least for the experience if not for shopping.

Købmagergade – Also a pedestrian shopping street in the same neighborhood as Strøget. Basically, the same concept as Strøget packet with popular global brands.

Pilestræde – Located behind Købmagergade, this popular shopping street is dotted with cozy cafes, funky bars, and trendy shops you will enjoy shopping in.

Elmegade – This is for the young at heart. The place is hip and trendy and vibrant. It is very close to Nørrebro's Sankt Hans Square and Nørrebrogade.

Jægersborggade – Located in the Nørrebro neighborhood, it is another buzzing and hip shopping area of Copenhagen with over 40 art galleries, vintage garment shops, jewelry shops displaying amazing designs, and more.

Malls:

There are three large shopping malls in Copenhagen:

Fisketorvet, Copenhagen Mall – located by the water and only one train-stop from Copenhagen Central Station. The mall holds 89 shops, 22 restaurants and coffee houses as well as one cinema.

Address: Kalvebod Brygge 59, 1560 København

Frederiksberg Centret – An award-winning shopping mall located two metro-stops from Nørreport station. The mall holds 90 shops and 6 high-quality eateries and coffee houses.

Address: Falkoner Alle 21, 2000 Frederiksberg

Field's – With 145 shops including 18 restaurants and coffee houses, Field's is the largest of the three malls. It's located a bit further outside the center in Ørestad (Amager), 7 metro stops from Nørreport station. Field's also holds a cinema.

Address: Arne Jacobsens Allé 12, 2300 København

Flea Markets:

These are set up during summer weekends, and there are many great ones around town. The flea markets in

Copenhagen are open between late May and early October.

For more information on the most popular flea markets: https://www.visitcopenhagen.com/copenhagen/flea-markets-copenhagen

Low budget stores

Flying Tiger

Flying Tiger is a Danish low-budget retail outlet that sells all sorts of low-priced items for as little as 10-30 DKR. Walking around in Flying Tiger is almost like going on a treasure hunt, and you might find yourself buying strange stuff you didn't know you needed. You will find decorations for your home, sunglasses, toys for the kids, creativity gear and umbrellas to name a very few. It's a trendy shop amongst locals as well as tourist and with more than 15 departments in Copenhagen, you don't have to look far to reach one.

Normal

"Normal" is a relatively new low budget retail outlet in Copenhagen which over the past few years has become very popular. "Normal" offers popular brands of daily necessity-products in a wide range such as shampoo, toothpaste, instant coffee, make-up and much else similar at meager prices. You might save 50% or even more in Normal compared to the regular grocery store across town.

Netto/Fakta/Rema1000

If you need groceries, Netto, Fakta, and Rema1000 are the discounted options that you will find all over the city, and usually they have a relatively good assortment of everyday groceries. However, they are not as well-stocked as the larger and more expensive supermarket such as Kvickly and Føtex.

14

Dining

In general, the quality of food in Copenhagen has risen in the past couple of decades. Pastries and street food have had true renaissances to name a few.

In this chapter, I will cover what Danish food you must try as well as some essential tips on eating out in Copenhagen.

Revel in the Joys of Street Food

Street food options are economical usually without compromising on quality and flavors.

In Copenhagen, Hot Dogs have been the preferred choice of street food for a long time. Now street food has had a real renaissance, and food markets have been popping up such as Torvehallerne and Reffen. These are some of the modern alternatives to the classic Danish street hot dog option at a pølsevogn.

The overall street food assortment in the city has increased, and both quality and healthy living are on the menu in many places.

Danish Foods You Must Try While in Copenhagen

Like in many other places and big cities of the world there is a considerable health trend wave in Copenhagen with one health-food eatery after the other popping up next to all the gyms. Traditional Danish food is not considered healthy in the modern sense of the word. However, the traditional cuisine is still alive and well. Here are the heavyweights that the Danes very much appreciate:

Pølser – The Danish version of American Hot Dogs, this dish is well-loved by the local Danes, and it would be criminal to come away from Copenhagen without trying it. Pølsevogne stand dot many streets in Copenhagen, and they are hard to miss. Pølser is usually served with mustard, ketchup, pickles, and some fries on the side.

Smørrebrød – These open-faced sandwiches are traditional and simplified Danish lunch dishes. These sandwiches are made typically with rye bread and topped with vegetables, raw shrimp or herring, meat or hard-boiled eggs. You must try a few varieties of smørrebrød.

Æbleskiver – These little round pancakes are part of the Danish Christmas traditions and usually served with some marmalade and sugar on the side. Very tasty indeed.

Wienerbrød – With a croissant-like consistency and filled with sugar and buttered cream, wienerbrød is a yummy sweet Danish dish. It is the wienerbrød that the Americans try to remake and call it "Danish pastry". However, what is available as Danish pastry in America is not the same.

Kartofler – There is not much classic Danish food served without potatoes, and no traditional Danish meal is really complete without a serving of kartofler. While they are cooked in different ways, the typical Danish way is to boil them and serve them along with meat and other vegetables. A sweet variety that is part of the Danish Christmas tradition is one that is cooked with sugar to create a lovely caramelized kartofler side dish.

Gløgg – A mulled wine that is flavored with various spices and orange and lemon peels, seasoned with little pieces of raisins and almonds. Gløgg is served warm and is a traditional accompaniment with æbleskiver during the Christmas season.

Risalamande – Somewhat similar to the rice pudding of America, it is topped with cherries and served cold. There is a tradition to serve this dish during Christmas. On Christmas eve there is an almond hidden in one of the risalamande bowls and the person who gets this 'treasure' without breaking it receives a reward or a prize.

Variety of Cheeses – Cheese factories and dairies are found all over Denmark and Copenhagen as well. A wide variety of cheeses are available here, and you must sample a few of them and, perhaps, purchase a couple to take home. The most common types of cheeses you can find in Copenhagen include Danbo, blue cheese, and Havarti. Cheese served on the side of fruit is a typical Danish food fashion often found as a dessert.

Where to Eat and Drink

Below I have included places at reasonable prices and worth going the extra mile for.

Coffee

Copenhagen has like most big cities a fair number of coffeehouses including Starbucks and the Danish counterpart "Espresso House". These both make decent coffees. However, if you want an extraordinary coffee experience, I recommend these places instead:

Roast Coffee

The coffee at Roast is made with a lot of effort and care. When you enter the small coffee house you will most likely be met with a genuinely friendly smile and greetings from the amicable staff, and you can rest assured, the coffee here is of the highest quality. It just tastes better, and it's not even very pricy.

Roast is located at Islands Brygge about 10-15 minutes' walk from Rådhuspladsen. If the weather allows, bringing your coffee to enjoy around the canal nearby is lovely.

Address: Vestmannagade 4, 2300 København

The Coffee Collective

The guys at The Coffee Collective take coffee making to another level. They have their own roastery and seek to perfect the coffee and unfold exceptional coffee experiences that also benefit the farmers across the globe. There are 4 Coffee Collective bars in Copenhagen.

Addresses:

Kristen Bernikows Gade 2, 1105 København K
Jægersborggade 57, 2200 København N
Godthåbsvej 34B, 2000 Frederiksberg,
Torvehallerne, Vendersgade 6D, 1363 København K

Danish Brunch

Mad og Kaffe

In Copenhagen, you will find plenty of restaurants serving brunch either as a buffet or a typical brunch plate. This doesn't happen at Mad og Kaffe. Here things are done a little differently. As a reasonably new restaurant, Mad og Kaffe has quickly become a popular brunch venue. You get to create your own brunch by ticking boxes at a card which the waiter then collects.

The dishes taste amazing, and the Copenhageners have discovered that! It is not unusual that a dedicated waiter will greet you at the door and put you on a waiting list along with the many others filling up space around the popular restaurant.

Mad og Kaffe is not a Danish restaurant in the traditional sense but an excellent example of modern Danish innovative cuisine. Very well worth the visit.

Tip: Arrive early especially on the weekends!

Addresses:

There are three Mad og Kaffe restaurants in Copenhagen:

Sønder Boulevard 68, 1720 København V
Tyrolsgade 6, 2300 København S
Godthåbsvej 45, 2000 Frederiksberg

Danish Lunch

Det Lille Apotek

Det Lille Apotek means "the Little Pharmacy". However, it doesn't provide you with medicine unless wholesome quality food can be regarded as such. It's a historical restaurant that dates all the way back to 1720! It's the oldest restaurant in all of Copenhagen and even H.C. Andersen used to be a regular customer at this facility. Of course, you should not miss this piece of Danish culture and hygge as well as traditional Danish cuisine. The menu is authentically Danish with a large selection of smørrebrød. If you are looking for modern health-based dishes, Det Lille Apotek is not your answer. But if you are going for an authentic hygge and a Danish cultural as well as historical food-experience I highly recommend Det Lille Apotek.

Address: Store Kannikestræde 15, 1169 København

Takeaway

WEDO

Delicious, healthy and with a great variety, WEDO has been nominated as the city's best takeaway (aok.dk). Choose a premade salad or make own of your own vegan or with meat or fish. Everything is made from scratch and WEDO is one of the Copenhageners favorite take-out. One they don't mind traveling a bit for if they don't live right in the neighborhood.

Addresses:

There are 5 WEDO shops in Copenhagen.

Kødbyen, Halmtorvet 21, 1700 København V
Jernbane Allé 39, 2720 Vanløse

Gammel Kongevej 176, 1850 Frederiksberg
Østerbrogade 151, 2100 København Ø
Valby Langgade 36, 2500 Valby

SMAG

SMAG (means "taste") is one of my favorite take-away places in town with reasonable prices. They offer sandwiches and a premade mixed salad buffet, and especially the salads are excellent. There are 3 different SMAG locations in Copenhagen

Addresses:

Fælledvej 25, 2200 Nørrebro
Nordre Frihavnsgade 13A, 2100 København Ø
Torvehallerne, Linnegade 17, 1361 København K

Itzi Pitzi

Frankly, the pizzas in Copenhagen are generally not of the highest standard, but there are exceptions.

Itzi Pitzi is an authentic Italian pizzeria with real Italien pizza makers behind the counter. It is a very tiny place, and they only do take-away, but the place is almost always crowded. Don't expect a high level of service but look forward to an unbelievably tasty pizza. If the weather allows you can sit on the grass right in front of Itzi Pitzi at Sønder Boulevard.

Address: Sønder Boulevard 51, 1720 København

Forno a Legna

Another tremendous Italian pizzeria is Forno a Legna in Frederiksberg. This is also trendy pizzeria among the Copenhageners with great tasting Italian pizzas and definitely worth a visit. It's possible to also sit down and enjoy your pizza at Forno a Legna.

Address: Falkoner Allé 42, 2000 Frederiksberg

Pastry

Pastry is truly a Danish delicacy. The Danish pastry shops have undergone a revival from being very uniform with little variety to being high quality and innovative bakeries.

Lagkagehuset

Lagkagehuset is an excellent place to try Danish Pastry. It's fair to say that it's the most popular bakery amongst the locals. Lagkagehuset is famous for their torts especially the Christianshavner Tort which is a delicate taste explosion. Copenhageners know and love Lagkagehuset for their high quality and innovative interpretation of bread and pastry. If you like dark rye bread (which is the type of bread most often used for smørrebrød), then Lagkagehuset also has some of the best in town. Their Chia-bread is my personal favorite.

Lagkagehuset also serves coffee and breakfast as well as delicious takeaway salad and sandwiches.

Tip: Don't ask for a "Danish pastry", nobody calls it that in Denmark.

A Few Tips on Eating Out in Copenhagen

Copenhagen is an expensive city and eating out can grab a big chunk of the budget. If cost is a factor for you, be on the lookout for eateries that serve the best fare at the most economical prices. Keep a lookout for 'buffet' services that offer a wide variety of Danish foods and at reasonable prices. Also, consider eating out at restaurants during lunch as opposed to dinner when the prices are a lot lower.

The tip amount is often included in the service charges of the bill. Yet, it is an unwritten and unspoken tipping etiquette to leave tips for the servers who make an effort especially at restaurants.

Velbekomme! (Enjoy!)

15

What do Locals Love?

The locals know the ins and outs of the city, what is worth spending time and money on and what isn't. In this chapter, you will learn the local's favorite spots. As you will see, many of them are also major tourist attractions included in the 3 Day must-see itinerary.

Their Bikes

The Copenhageners ride their bicycle to get around everywhere. The city is no bigger than you can easily bike around to almost everything. There are plenty of opportunities for renting a bike in the city, and some of them are even electric for a faster more comfortable ride.

The Locals' Favorite Spots

Islands Brygge Harbor Bath

Islands Brygge is a beautiful canal quay situated on the coast of Amager close to the city center. Only 10 minutes' walk from Town Hall Square. Constructed in the 1880s, Islands Brygge is today a trendy place to relax with a glass of beer, especially during the summer. You can simply stroll along the canal, even jump in for a refreshing swim at the clean harbor bath. It is usually populated with the young and hip crowd of Copenhagen, and it's a place where you can mingle easily with the locals. In summer there are frequently flea markets along the canal.

The harbor bath built right in the middle of the city is a sight for sore eyes, especially during summer. The perfectionism of Danish culture is evident here because the authorities check for the quality of water at this place before allowing anyone to dive in! A well-maintained lawn in front of the pool is perfect for ball games, for a picnic, or simply to sunbathe with a book in hand. Expect it to be jam-packed on any hot day.

Amager Strandpark

This vast public beach park has fast become one of the Copenhageners favorite city getaway spots in the summer. It's safe to say that Amager Strand is the number one beach-choice among locals. It was artificially recreated in 2005 by adding a 1.2 miles island which gave the beach a renaissance, and today the seaside park is used by runners, swimmers, kayakers, segwayers, skateboarders and roller skaters besides the obvious sunbathing and picnicking guests. Around 1 million people visit the beach every year.

It is located not far from the city center only a 10 minutes metro ride from Nørreport St.

The Lakes

The Lakes are primarily used for recreational purposes such as walking and running around them. They consist of 3 lakes situated in a row – altogether 5 basins with a distance of 4 miles all around.

The Lakes are one of the favorite areas for locals to go for a recreational walk or run.

It's possible to rent a paddle boat to enjoy a trip for two on the lakes. This is usually an activity more often enjoyed by tourists though.

Tivoli

The Danes love Tivoli. It's typical for a Dane to own a season-pass, and Tivoli has something wonderful to offer both summer and winter. In summer there is a free pop/rock concert every Friday called "Fredagsrock" (Friday Rock) with popular national and international band-names that leaves the park packed with people.

In winter the amusement park is transformed into a Christmas wonderland with beautiful Christmas lights and decorations all around. It is like walking around in a fairytale and should you visit Copenhagen around Christmas it is highly recommendable to experience this almost magical adventure. Remember to dress warmly, it is cold, and all of the experience takes place outdoors.

The locals are particularly fond of "Friday Rock" in summer and "Tivoli Winter Market" in winter.

Reffen

The Copenhageners have really embraced the concept of street food mekkas in recent years, and the recently opened Reffen (May 2018) is no exception. Even though the location of Reffen is a bit outside of Copenhagen city center, the locals still like to go for an afternoon of "hang out" at Reffen during the summer.

Kødbyen (The Meatpacking District)

Kødbyen offers a variety of restaurants, bars, nightclubs, and art galleries. It's for the hip and the cool and one of - if not the most – popular areas for a night out among the locals especially the young. Kødbyen is a slice of contemporary Copenhagen of today and a tourist gem since it's not at all filled with people expecting to get a share of tourists' travel budget.

The Parks: Fælledparken, Frederiksberg Have, Kongens Have, Ørstedsparken

Copenhageners love their parks. The parks serve as sanctuaries for the locals living in the city apartments year around. Groups, as well as individuals, use the parks as their everyday getaway. You will find families having a picnic, people sunbathing, youngsters playing ball or frisbee and locals running to stay fit. Enjoy some people watching while having a picnic in one of the parks, that's a very local-like activity.

Torvehallerne

Currently, Copenhagen has just one indoors food market, and it is widely popular. 115.000 local Copenhageners visit the market every week. Torvehallerne offers more than 60 stands with a great variety of fresh, high-quality convenience food and delicacies as well as take-away and non-food stands. You can enjoy a delicious meal at one of the stands or perhaps bring food or drinks to enjoy outside at the nearby lakes or one of the parks. The freshness, the quality, and the great variety of delicacies are primary factors in the success of Torvehallerne ever since it opened up in 2011.

Værnedamsvej

Værnedamsvej is one of the locals' favorite streets because of its charming atmosphere, unique boutiques, and cozy bars and restaurants. It is not a long street quite the contrary, but it is unlike any other street in Copenhagen. This street is not often known amongst tourist as it is a bit out of the way from the main tourist attractions.

16

Connecting with the Locals - Etiquette and Socializing

One of the most rewarding experiences when visiting a foreign country is meeting and getting to know the locals. Also, it's obviously helpful for things to go smoothly when visiting a big city in foreign lands, so knowing the etiquette and peculiar norms of a country are imperative.

I have dedicated this chapter to the ins and outs of breaking boundary with the Copenhageners and added some etiquette tips that the Danes hold dear to heart.

By being aware of the "rules" and following them, you are opening your heart and mind in such a way that you will not only come across as friendly to the Danes but also as a person who appreciates the nuances of living within the framework of a society that is different to your own. Danes value this a lot.

Icebreakers

Talking About the Weather

Danish people talk about the weather a lot especially with someone they don't know so well. It's one of the main icebreakers, and you can be sure to connect at least a little with a Dane if you discuss the weather. It's a bit of a contradictory subject though. In theory, Danes believe it is a very trivial even boring subject and that it represents shallowness and lack of creativity to talk about it. However, it is frequently discussed, and it's an easy and excepted icebreaker. Because the Danish weather is really unpredictable, it often seems obvious to mention it.

Humor

Danes love humor and self-irony. Making some fun of yourself is usually considered very charming. If you are trying your way in funny-land, be careful not to offend anybody. A stand-up comedian at a stage can get away with a lot more than regular people having regular conversations, especially with strangers. If you have a suitable non-offensive joke at hand it could be a great icebreaker.

Humility

Danes definitely appreciate true humility and respond very well to polite and humble requests as opposed to a demanding self-important attitude. Simple mannered phrases such as "sorry", "excuse me" and "thank you" are highly appreciated amongst the locals and will get you a long way. This might seem obvious to the majority, but it's just worth keeping in mind if you need to ask for direction, etc.

What Are Danes Like?

The following breakdown of what Danish people are like is a rough generalizing which capture some cultural tendencies.

Danes are generally very healthy, perhaps, driven by the general feeling of contentment among the people. Undoubtedly helped immensely by the clean air, free medical care, a balanced and well working social system and a high level of fresh food products.

The Danes are generally pretty trusting towards each other. There is a strong sense of fairness, and even though Danes mind their own business a lot, there is also consensus that it's the right thing to help each other out.

Even in a place like Christiania that does not entirely come under the laws and regulations of the city, you will not easily find disorderliness or mayhem or unruliness. In general, Danes are designed to follow the rules without having to be policed by law enforcement agencies.

In general Danes are well-mannered, however, watch out in traffic. This is where Danes run amok and sometimes really let the temper out towards one another. That doesn't happen all the time but more often than in other situations.

Oh, and if you happen to be famous, Danish people are known for respecting other's privacy in public and leaving actors and other famed ones alone on the streets. Danes will look and perhaps point, but not often approach the (poor) famous people.

Danish Etiquette Tips

These tips might not all be relevant for a short stay in Copenhagen. However, if you are invited for a meal or dinner by a local, remembering the following salient points will get you a long way:

Punctuality - The Danes take punctuality seriously, and if you are not on time, then it is considered a rude gesture not easily forgiven. If your invitations say 1800 hours, then the maximum leeway is 1805, no later; a few minutes earlier than the scheduled time is fine but not late. But if you are going to be late by that permitted five minutes, Danish etiquette mandates you to call and inform your host about the delay.

Don't worry too much, you have an out: It is considered good manners to apologize for being late should it happen, and by offering an apology and an explanation you will be forgiven, and peace will be restored.

Gifts – You should not come empty-handed to your host's house. Carrying a gift for him or her is good manners. Any small gift like nice chocolate or flowers or a bottle of wine is fine. It doesn't have to be wrapped, it's the thought and gesture that counts the most.

Shoes – If you enter a private house, remember to ask your host if you should take off your shoes. Some Danes have strong opinions about this and don't allow shoes inside their home. Others don't mind. This varies a lot so always ask.

Introductions and Greeting – It is up to you to take the first step and introduce yourself to the people present at the gathering individually greeting each of them in turn. A handshake is a common form of greeting in a social group, and a handshake is appropriate if you don't know someone. Hugging is not customary unless you have met before. Already the second time you meet a person you can consider giving a hug, that would usually not be out of line in private events. Danes don't often kiss on the cheek when meeting up. It happens, but it's rare.

In Denmark, you greet everyone using their first names. Titles like Mr., Mrs., or Miss are rarely used. Women and men are treated as equals, and outward symbols of 'gentleman chivalry' are not very becoming in Danish culture. Touching someone's arm or shoulder during a conversation is also not customary in Denmark.

Seating Etiquette – When you are called for dinner (if it is a sit-down affair), you must find your allocated seat at the table. There could be table cards, or the host will guide you to your seat. You remain standing at your designated place behind the chair until all come to the table and stand at their proper designated places. When the host announces, Velbekomme or Værs'go, this is when you have his or her permission to sit down along with the others.

Dress – Casual dress is an accepted way of dressing in Denmark. Formal suits and ties are not a pre-requisite even for formal meetings.

Thanking Your Host for the Food – If you are invited for a meal (breakfast, lunch or dinner) remember to thank your host for the food before leaving the table. This is customary amongst Danes, and it is actually considered rude not to.

Thanking Your Host Before Leaving – This is mandatory etiquette. You must find your host when you are ready to leave and thank him or her for a wonderful time and then take leave. Politeness is an essential etiquette in Danish culture. Although there is no word that means 'please' in the Danish language, 'tak' (=thank you) is very often used and is expected from everyone as well.

Getting Personal – The Danes can take a long time to build personal rapport. So, while you must be polite and courteous, getting too personal at the first meeting is usually frowned upon. Once you get to know a person really well, then the Danes make great friends. They hold their social circle very tight, and you might have to work hard to earn a spot in the tight network.

Socializing Among the Danes

The Danes do not socialize quite the same way as the Americans and the English who more often hang out together after office hours for a drink or coffee. It can happen but not as often. So, if you ask a Dane out for coffee and he or she declines the invitation, then don't feel bad. That is how Danes behave. There are a lot of family obligations that come first before socializing. Danes usually have preset schedules and don't often like to or want to change the routines without a purpose (other than socializing).

17

Outro

I hope you got a lot out of this guide and feel ready to explore Copenhagen.

As I mentioned in the beginning, proper planning ahead of your stay is time-saving and imperative for a short stay. However, researching a city extensively before going could be a disadvantage. Once you are in Copenhagen, I invite you to forget all your research and what you think you know and experience it all with fresh eyes and a totally open mind.

So, now and lastly, I will invite you to clear your head and open your heart, mind, and soul to the diversity that

Copenhagen has to offer a traveler who comes to her doorstep for great adventure.

Tak fordi du læste med og rigtig god rejse!

P.S. Cheers is "skål" in Danish. That's a good one to know.

Made in the USA
Coppell, TX
08 November 2019